Seaside

Katie Dicker

Published by Evans Brothers Limited
2A Portman Mansions
Chiltern Street
London W1U 6NR

© Evans Brothers Limited 2009

Produced for Evans Brothers Limited by
White-Thomson Publishing Ltd

Printed in China by New Era Printing Co. Ltd
Printed on chlorine-free paper from sustainably managed sources.

Educational consultant: Sue Palmer MEd FRSA FEA
Project manager: Katie Dicker
Picture research: Amy Sparks
Design: Balley Design Limited
Creative director: Simon Balley
Designer/Illustrator: Andrew Li

For Edward

British Library Cataloguing in Publication Data

Dicker, Katie
  Seaside. - (Out and about) (Sparklers)
  1. Seashore - Juvenile literature 2. Seaside resorts -
  Juvenile literature
  I. Title
  910.9'146

ISBN: 978 0 2375 3875 0

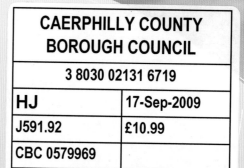

Contents

Day trip

Quick!

Let's go!

Come with us to the seaside!

4

Sand and pebbles

This sand is good for building.

bucket

How TALL can you make

a pile of pebbles?

balancing

7

Seaweed and shells

What different types of shells can you find?

itchy!

What does **seaweed feel** like?

9

In the water

piggy back

The sea water is cool on a hot day.

10

Wind and waves

A windy day is good for surfing on the waves.

13

Rockpools

At low tide, this beach is full of rockpools.

14

How do these rockpool

creatures move?

Now make a shape like a starfish!

17

Fishing

These boats are used to catch fish at sea.

fishing rod

What would YOU use to catch fish from the pier?

19

What's YOUR favourite seaside game?

Heeeeave!

21

Notes for adults

Sparklers books are designed to support and extend the learning of young children. The **Food We Eat** titles won a Practical Pre-School Silver Award and the **Body Moves** titles won a Practical Pre-School Gold Award. The books' high-interest subjects link in to the Early Years curriculum and beyond. Find out more about Early Years and reading with children from the National Literacy Trust (www.literacytrust.org.uk).

Themed titles
Seaside is one of four **Out and About** titles that encourage children to explore outdoor spaces. The other titles are:
Park   Garden   Wood

A CD to accompany the series (available from Evans Publishing Group tel 020 7487 0920 or email sales@evansbrothers.co.uk) provides sound effects from each environment, as well as popular songs and rhymes that relate to outdoor exploration.

Areas of learning
Each **Out and About** title helps to support the following Foundation Stage areas of learning:
Personal, Social and Emotional Development
Communication, Language and Literacy
Mathematical Development
Knowledge and Understanding of the World
Physical Development
Creative Development

Making the most of reading time
When reading with younger children, take time to explore the pictures together. Ask children to find, identify, count or describe different objects. Point out colours and textures. Allow quiet spaces in your reading so that children can ask questions or repeat your words. Try pausing mid-sentence so that children can predict the next word. This sort of participation develops early reading skills.

Follow the words with your finger as you read. The main text is in Infant Sassoon, a clear, friendly font designed for children learning to read and write. The labels and sound effects add fun and give the opportunity to distinguish between levels of communication. Where appropriate, labels, sound effects or main text may be presented phonically. Encourage children to imitate the sounds.

As you read the book, you can also take the opportunity to talk about the book itself with appropriate vocabulary such as "page", "cover", "back", "front", "photograph", "label" and "page number".

You can also extend children's learning by using the books as a springboard for discussion and further activities. There are a few suggestions on the facing page.

Pages 4–5: Day trip

Explain to children that the seaside is a place where the land meets the sea. Show them different stretches of coastline on a map. You could take children to a local beach to experience the seaside for themselves. Alternatively, you could make your own beach. Fill a tray (three-quarters) with sand or pebbles and add a plastic divider. Add 'sea' water and move the tray back and forth to make waves.

Pages 6–7: Sand and pebbles

Children may enjoy looking for stones with special shapes or markings – at the beach or from a collection of pebbles. Help the children to make a paperweight by varnishing their stones. Children may also enjoy activities at the beach, such as throwing small pebbles into the water, knocking a tin can off a pile of stones or making a sand boat.

Pages 8–9: Seaweed and shells

Encourage children to collect seashells and group them in colour or order of size. Use books or the Internet to help the children identify where the shells come from. You could also collect some dried seaweed. Draw a face on a piece of card and use shells for the features and seaweed as 'hair'.

Pages 10–11: In the water

Children may enjoy making their own sunglasses, sun hat or arm bands from card and tissue paper. Talk to children about the importance of water and sun safety at the seaside. What other safety precautions are important? What behaviour makes the seaside a safe place for others to use?

Pages 12–13: Wind and waves

Children may enjoy playing a game about waves. Ask the children to hold the edges of a blue sheet and to make 'waves' by slowly moving the sheet up and down. Children take it in turns to run underneath the sheet without being caught by the waves. Children may also enjoy making their own coloured kite or windmill to use on a windy day.

Pages 14–15: Rockpools

Help children to make their own rockpool in a tray of water, and their own rockpool creatures using self-hardening clay and waterproof paint. Children could play a game by hiding the creatures in their rockpool and asking a friend to find the different animals.

Pages 16–17: Sealife

Collect a series of photographs of seaside creatures, cut from magazines or printed from the Internet. Make a collage of your creatures on the wall, creating an 'underwater' effect with blue and green tissue paper. Use books or the Internet to help the children identify the different creatures.

Pages 18–19: Fishing

Encourage children to draw a seaside picture with sand, sea and sky. Help them to cut a slit for the horizon. Children could make their own boats from card with a thin strip from the hull as a handle. Put the boats 'through' the horizon to show them 'bobbing' along the water. Children may also enjoy making their own fishing rods or nets from strong card and string.

Pages 20–21: Fun and games

Children may enjoy acting out a day at the seaside. Encourage children to make the sounds of the sea or the seagulls, to walk barefoot and to act out feeling hot in the sun. Children may also enjoy drawing a postcard about a day at the beach, talking about the games they played, the sights they saw and the sounds they heard.

Index

Picture acknowledgements:
Alamy: 10 (ACE Stock Limited), 18 (PCL); **Corbis:** 9 (Paul Barton/zefa), 11 (Paul Barton/zefa), 17 (Randy Faris), 21 (Rolf Bruderer); **Getty Images:** cover girls (Stockbyte), 6 (Jose Luis Pelaez Inc), 13 (Stockbyte), 14 (Joson Photo LLC), 19 (Christopher Robbins), 20 (Gallo Images/Guy Bubb); **IStockphoto:** cover beach (Alberto Pomares), cover sky (JLF Capture), 15 starfish, 15 anemone, 15 limpet; **Photolibrary:** 8 (Santa Clara); **Shutterstock:** 2–3 beach (Christian Wheatley), 4 (Monkey Business Images), 5 (Mikhail Tchkheidze), 7 (Jozsef Szasz-Fabian), 12 (sculpies), 15 crab (Lijuan Guo), 16 (Manuel Fernandes), 22–23 beach (Christian Wheatley), 24 beach (Christian Wheatley).